# Pretty Nearly All Natural

*poems by*

# Genie Abrams

*Finishing Line Press*
Georgetown, Kentucky

# Pretty Nearly All Natural

Copyright © 2024 by Genie Abrams
ISBN 979-8-88838-739-9 First Edition
All rights reserved under International and Pan-American Copyright Conventions. No part of this book may be reproduced in any manner whatsoever without written permission from the publisher, except in the case of brief quotations embodied in critical articles and reviews.

Publisher: Leah Huete de Maines
Editor: Christen Kincaid
Cover Art: Genie Abrams
Author Photo: Timothy J. Riss
Cover Design: Elizabeth Maines McCleavy

Order online: www.finishinglinepress.com
Also available on GoldenHourBookstore.com, Barnes and Noble or amazon.com.

Author inquiries and mail orders:
Finishing Line Press
PO Box 1626
Georgetown, Kentucky 40324
USA

# Contents

Women ..................................................................................................1
Writer's Block: Blame the Grackles ..................................................2
The Lord of Exit 23 ............................................................................3
Triolet on Gardens in October ..........................................................4
Mowing in November ........................................................................5
Stopping to Compare Frosts on a Snowy Evening ..........................6
Autumn Sestina ..................................................................................7
December ............................................................................................8
Vegetable Breakdown ........................................................................9
Solstice Villanelle ..............................................................................10
Crows ................................................................................................11
We Come to Work (at the DMV) ....................................................12
Laggards ............................................................................................13
The Mourner ....................................................................................14
The Quarter ......................................................................................15
The Gift ............................................................................................17
Two Dead in Blaze ............................................................................18
Reporter's Lament ............................................................................19
Annuals ............................................................................................20
Native American Perennials ............................................................21
Late-Winter Cryptography ..............................................................23
Forward March ................................................................................24
Relief ..................................................................................................25
None of Us in Nineveh ....................................................................26
Against Roses ....................................................................................27
Summer Run ....................................................................................28
Silly Sonnet ......................................................................................29
Doing the Dishes with my Father ..................................................30
But the Trees ....................................................................................31
Come Sit on the Porch ....................................................................32
The Rights of Nature ......................................................................33
Preserve Me ......................................................................................34

**Women**

I sleep awash in moonlight and plants.
The ivies, curtaining my bedroom window,
cast lacy shadows across my face,
and the full moon calls us all.
I swear I can hear the damp, undulant roots creeping downward
through the holes in their containers,
beckoning me in their moist, urgent language.
Or am I dreaming? But I have not dreamt like this in a month.

The leathery old snake-plant in her clay pot on the sill
stiffens as a moonbeam strikes her spiky shoots.
They are engorged with new life,
transfused into the arms of a child
pleading to be lifted,
crying:
Take me, mother.

The purple passion seethes in reds and blues:
I toss beneath the fury of her furry tendrils. Nothing sleeps tonight.
The succulents' jammy juices burst into sticky pearls through the tips
of their thick fingers, while the wandering Jew
waves her thin leaves
in a languorous adieu.

The night parses my dreams and tugs at my blood like the tides:
The African violet and cyclamen know this is lunacy.
I stare, sleepless, at the moon through the blood-red braids
that suspend the crimson coleus above my bed,
and give myself up to her enchantment.

When I awake,
I greet my period.

**Writer's Block: Blame the Grackles**

Grackles gleam in their blue-black suits
under the feeder. Their constant, clanging clamor
ruins each attempt of mine to hammer
out a phrase or two; each cry refutes
reason. All that senseless, jangling yammer
shoots thought to scattered shreds and loots
logic's tattered pockets; forget grammar.
Where was I? Hopping quick among the roots,
they race to grab the seeds and stammer
shrilly, never heeding if I am, or
maybe not, amused at hell's recruits.
Yet as each noisy, black-beaked bastard quits,
a blank page still accuses my poor wits.

**The Lord of Exit 23**

As grey and gnarly sticks, your jagged throne,
thrust against the morning mist and tear it,
you pierce the frosty air with gaze unguessed,
and trust that we commuter-fools can bear it.
We don't look up: We're blind and blank below.
And through a thousand sighs, with wizened eyes
and withered souls we fumble for our tolls
and go about the day not well nor wise.

We lurch in lurid traffic toward our rackets,
but you don't mind that slugs can't hear you sing.
All unadored, you work your wheeling sunward,
there to seek the worthy of your wing.

Big bird, brown bird, beam a blessing downward;
sail in silent spiral for your soul's nobility.
Fly your holy arc above the featherless and feeble
and commute this working-day, and set me free.

Your grace, the soar and swoop of you, the might,
the awesome flight, your sacred scope and see
proclaim that you alone will reign forever,
O red-tailed Lord of Exit Twenty-Three.

**Triolet on Gardens in October**

All mums and asters, asters and mums:
Summer's wild wisdom has withered and died.
Oh, it's all but appalling how autumn comes
all mums and asters, asters and mums.
This early darkness nips and numbs
my dahlias—my daisies! Now I must abide
all mums and asters, asters and mums:
Summer's wild wisdom has withered and died.

**Mowing in November**

Pushing the power mower over our weedy, rocky lawn, I wonder:
How long before I run out of gas? This yard is riddled with ruts,
nuts, stones, twigs, holes, ridges, bumps ... You can't mow it fast.
Even a young person can't mow it fast. But I'm old now,
and I fear I'm going to run out of gas before I finish my work.
It's November. A breeze is rising; clouds are whipping past.
In the distance, hills are fall-colored; the river cold as steel.
Now I play my silent game: Will I run out before I reach the feeder?
Will I get past the porch, or make it, with God's grace, all the way to the walk?
What about the strip we own across the street—will I get that far?
When I reach the rusted barrow (my silly, pink-painted planter),
I look back and think, if I run out here, I'll be satisfied: I'll have done the bulk of it
and have nothing to be embarrassed about.
When you're mowing for the last time, the manual says, you should just keep going 'til you run out of gas.
For once, I'm following instructions.

**Stopping to Compare Frosts on a Snowy Evening**

The river gleams with virgin snow.
I can't appreciate it, though:
The cold has bitten through my ears
and left my car in need of tow.

Upstate winters, these late years,
are not the ones my heart reveres.
I want to write my poems in peace,
and not face furnace-failure fears.

I wish the icy sleet would cease,
and I could see returning geese,
instead of birds all headed back
to milder clime and fairer lease.

Someday, I'll join that southbound pack,
when southbound trains come down the track:
As Frosts go, Robert clobbers Jack;
As Frosts go, Robert clobbers Jack.

**Autumn Sestina**

The breezes break the brittle garnet leaves
and shake them on their desultory way.
Stems tickle stone and lawn, then lightly lift
again, like kites on afternoons of sun
when school is out, and kids are unaware
of all that lies ahead—the pain, the blows,
       the office tedium, the drear that blows
       through bleaker days and disappoints and leaves
       the grownups vaguely scared. All unaware,
       kids fashion forts to play in on their way;
       they glory, while they can, the fading sun
       and float atop distraction's famous lift.
The bitter, brilliant winds of winter lift
the skirts of trees. A chill descends and blows
across the town. Our gazes seek the sun
that rises late, reluctant. Then it leaves,
as if repulsed, to somehow find its way
to warmer, better climes. We're unaware
       that icicles can leave us unaware
       of other seasons, other days that lift
       the sun and raise our hopes. Another way
       is time itself: A comfort comes that blows,
       at last, a kinder breeze—a thing that leaves
       us feeling that, as born again, the sun

may yet revive the grass and greens. The sun
dares spring above the chimneys, unaware
of how its warmth, rejuvenated, leaves
a sprig of gaiety in greyed-out hearts. To lift
our spirits from the tomb, a zephyr blows
a shofar-blast that shepherds in a way
       of thinking new to us—a brighter way
       of seeing birds and buds, and even sun
       again, when we had given up. The blows
       we suffered—snow and sleet—all unaware
       of these are we, when warming breezes lift
       the vegetation up from mud and leaves.
With hidden sun, our hearts are unaware.
Hold onto hope—the only way to lift
us from the icy blows and fallen leaves.

**December**

Sleet slanting in sheets,
flinging tiny wet diamonds all over the streets,
and wind banging our wraps
like the beat of a drummer attacking his traps:
Hell's howling tonight,
while we await days that are "merry and bright."

**Vegetable Breakdown**

Suddenly
it has become very important to me
to remember the name of the vegetable
I am holding in my hand.
Obsessed with consumption, consumed with obsession, I will
let the water run, let the timer buzz, let the phone ring,
suspend the world in its moment,
this peeler in my other hand forever,
and gape unbreathing, immobile,
immortalized by a vegetable.

Thus will I learn to concentrate, to keep my mind with me
and not to do things mindlessly anymore.
Because there's something wrong with me:
I can't pay attention. I'm losing my words.

Think …
This vegetable is mocking me.
It's wincing with the effort of not laughing out loud. It's the …
Not the thing the Irish eat, the potato, but the …
Think.

My fear, you see, is it means something about me—
about my life, and the way I live.
And I know what it is: It's this living-alone business.
And so I must take this witness, this vegetable,
and hide it, or burn it. Turnip.
Turnip! That's it!

Now the world and its words are returning;
my synapses, firing away.
Forgive me, folks; a momentary lapse.
Go about your business.

(Hah! I may be crazy,
but I know my vegetables.)

**Solstice Villanelle**

Winter-afternoon light on the street
Palls the day with feeble flakes and frost:
All is icy gutter-mud and sleet.

Now December's darking days repeat.
No one even dreams of summers lost:
Winter-afternoon light on the street.

Dirty puddles dampening our feet,
Sooty snowbanks greyed by bus exhaust:
All is icy gutter-mud and sleet.

Swirling trash and biting winds complete
The awful scene as fading light is lost:
Winter-afternoon light on the street.

Who recalls the sunny das when heat
Glorified our bones, and lightly cost?
All is icy gutter-mud and sleet.

It seems that gloom is long and light is fleet,
With soggy Solstice day so newly crossed.
Winter-afternoon light on the street:
All is icy gutter-mud and sleet.

**Crows**

They muster at dusk by the river;
they caucus along the dark limbs.
Their awful shofars play appalling
    funereal hymns.

They hawk us their merchandise boldly;
they want us to look at their wares,
but care not to whom they are calling
    as darkness ensnares.

Like graduates' wild celebrations
their raucous arrival begins
ever louder, incessantly bawling
    competitive dins.

They squawk us their mad, raspy gossip,
each screeching its need to be heard:
Caw-caw clogs the air with a galling
    mock of the word.

But now all the crow-talk is fading,
and dots of jet dapple the oaks.
Night finds their feathers enthralling
    and matches their cloaks.

### We Come to Work (at the DMV)

We work. We take our tea.
We pass the time most pleasantly,
and we ask after our families.
And we type.

We talk about the weather or the parking,
and now and then we cannot help remarking
that we like our situations. And we type
(though what we type is, very often, tripe).

Oh, it's not quite what you'd care for,
but it's money we are there for—
the money, and the coffee, the fellowship, the tea,
the politics, the gossip and the hype.

See, it's not so much a job as 'tis a rhythm,
and if you're not against 'em, then you're with 'em—
my comrades, my buddies, my pals,
my colleagues and my crones—in short, "the gals."

We are not fast; we are not slow. But we like the way we go,
and we got everything an office wants:
the cookies and the copier, the coffee and the clock,
and the gossip and the lovely ambiance.

And it occupies our fingers, and now and then our minds,
and we eat the cheese they send us and we throw away the rinds.
So if you peek into our office, do not sneer; do not smirk.
And it you look in on us and we're not worn to a frazzle,
well, we do not come to dazzle: We come to work.

**Laggards**

Cats lounge on the brownstone sill
all the damp spring morning,
their tails the quote and end-quote
of my uncomposed thoughts.
They give me a nod, vague in the fog,
as they knead their pebbled perch.
I am on my way to work,
and the madness of fluorescence,
and the comfort of coffee,
while the coffee-colored cat
and the grey cat
lounge.

There I will pull the paper from the printer
and wait for words to rescue me.
And I will stamp, "Must!" and "Urgent!"
on one hundred bits of paper, while back home,
the cats' tails dangle into their own perfect letters:
the "e" and the "g," for example.
There is much in what they say,
and much in what they don't say.

Trapped in a place of no shade and no shadows
there at the Musak-mill
where every cable, cord, phone and fixture hums,
ill-pitched and shrill,
erasing memory of all things felt, heard, tasted, seen,
scented, sensed and loved,
not 'til I've wrapped my hands around a warm cup
and threaded my thumbs through its handle
will I recall the leafy, still street
where the placid cats pad
on the gritty sill.

Some day, I think, I will not go to work.
I will sit on the stoop
with two heavy cats in my lap,
feeling their delicate bones
and learning what I can
through the soft fur
and the soft skin
all the quiet morning.

**The Mourner**

The cat is dead; I need a new cat.

For now I am alone, crocheting in the bath
with no cat to catch at my yarn and hook.
I don't miss her at all.

Sometimes I think about the rat who hit my cat.
They say he didn't stop; must not have heard the splat.
And I wonder if the cat felt sentimental at all,
about her life,
as she died.

I wonder if she had regrets.

I should have asked the neighbor-children
more questions about the circumstances.
All I had was the report of the eight-year-old:
"Snarf got hit by a motorcycle."
I should have more curiosity. I'm not normal.
I didn't even go into the yard to see where they buried her,
and now they're mad. I just said, "No;
thank you, though."
All these years, I haven't once asked
where my mother's ashes are.

The kids who found my cat burned to tell me
how they peeled her from the street and dug her grave.
Now they want to make a cross for her.
When they came to my door
to ask for "twine, or tape," I gave them tape,
but when they added sweetly, "Want to know why we need it?
What we're making for your cat?"
I just said, "No. No, I don't." They hate me for that.

The cat is dead; I need a new cat.

## The Quarter

> *I've lost my quarter, darn it. I dropped it in the snow.*
> *By now, I should have found it—it was sixty years ago.*

The snow was already a foot deep
and now sleet was pelting us on our way to school.
I trailed my brother and sister, deliberately.
Our dad had given me (and not Dave or Val) a quarter—
a shiny new one. (Or does it shine only in my memory?)
That meant I could have an ice-cream sandwich with lunch,
and get one for my friend Sharon, too, and still have a nickel!
Flipping my quarter with each booted step, I was overjoyed. My soul expanded.
I lost myself in imagining: "Hey, Sharon! I got a quarter!
Want an ice-cream sandwich? I'll buy you one!"
I would be so happy to make her happy.
Both our families were kind of poor. She had no father; we had no mom.

Among fifth-graders on the playground, I was always the first one
chosen. I could hit, run, throw, catch, dribble, spin,
and shoot better than anyone in Miss McAfee's, even the boys.

At home, I was cook and comedian. My job was to make us all
food and happy. I would flip not just pancakes,
but also the spatula itself. I'd send it high enough to almost graze the ceiling,
while I waited for the bubbles to sizzle just right in the pan.
The whole family—Dad, Dave and Val—laughed and applauded.
I'd send it on a triple-flip, dripping bits of melted butter.
I'd spin three-sixty and still catch it nonchalantly, waist-high. I never missed.

Now sleet noisily intruded into my happiness.
One last time, I flipped my wet quarter from a stiff mitten.
And missed. My smile and I both froze.
It pierced the bubbly snow somewhere silent, edgewise.
Dave turned and yelled from the top of the hill, "Come on! We'll be late!"
I trudged upward knowing a new kind of numb.
Finding that quarter would be like finding
the place where you'd stabbed the ocean with a knife.

Oh, I hope some kid found it years ago, while playing.
I do. But I'm just saying:
If you happen to see an old quarter lying at the edge of the park near Farrington and Dubois, would you let me know?

**The Gift**

Today I stumbled on my mother's name
inside an old book, in her youthful hand.
Her fountain pen forever would proclaim
her future as a writer, proudly planned.
My fevered calculations had her ten
or twelve years old, at most, when first she read
that book about a writer and the men
she loved, and how she found the one she wed.
Inked initials on one yellowed page
ordain her "REW"—an ancient word for sorrow.
And Ruth she was, and rueful at the age
of forty, when she died, more grief to borrow.
And yet she left, in melancholy guise,
this joyful gift—this sepia surprise.

**Preserve Me**

Sorbitol, mannitol, xylitol too—and here's more stuff on which to chew:
cellulose fiber, cellulose gum, carageenan (yum yum yum),
aspartame with citric acid (*mangia*, please: approval's tacit),
glucose, fructose, sucrose, more; polydextrose (Keeping score?),
maltitol benzene? And what the hell's "datem"? You hardly know just
    how to rate 'em.
Mono- and di-glycerides; can we ever stem the tides?
BHA and BHT; guar gum for you and me;
and calcium proprionate (I can't believe what I just ate).
Labels ladle out advice they want us all to follow,
but always add a grain of salt—and then don't swallow.

**Two Dead in Blaze**

Disc jockeys die queerly
as the radio station burns in winter.
They thud to the hard rock walk four flights below,
absurd, flaming ice-balls, and it's too cold to snow.
The reporter only knows she wants to go.
"Christ," someone says, and someone else says, "Ten below."

On impact, the DJs shatter.
The weather has them brittle as a platter.
Splintered glass glitters in the beds of their charred, bare skin,
and shards of their joints and their battered bones point
across the knobs of spines to the reporter.

Her breath fogs the focus-glass: She can't remember why she's there.
The film-advance lever snaps in her mittened hand.
"This is not being recorded," she thinks, and just recently she'd care,
but not while she stands in the razor-wind,
face cut by gusts of ten-below air.

The busted boys are naked. The reporter wants to know
why disc jockeys would be naked in the winter,
in the red and ruined snow.
But now the firemen come, while from inside somewhere,
still the demented jingle, the Number-One single blare.

They try to pry them from the ice: No luck.
They stick, like the water is stuck in the hoses,
and reporters in poses they don't understand,
while stars and cops' bubble-lights
freeze moments the reporter too clearly sees
silently piercing our lives
like pricks from the tips of invisible picks
so fine that, for the longest time,
you feel nothing—nothing at all.

**Reporter's Lament**

Whether they're deathless or already dead,
our glorious stories are only once-read.
For all that we dream of and all that we wish,
tomorrow's editions wrap yesterday's fish.

**Annuals**

October's here, and time to let it go.
Ridiculous to think more fruit will come;
you cannot gather flowers in the snow,
nor add another crop to summer's sum.

Bold autumn will not deign to hesitate,
withholding wicked winds and slashing sleet.
To hope a buried seed will germinate,
or bud will bloom, is folly; no repeat.

And yet a bee is buzzing on the petal,
a leaf is left upon the slender stem,
and seeing these, I know I'll never settle
upon a day to say goodbye to them.

Perhaps they're telling me (reminder wry)
the season nears when I, myself, go by.

**Native American Perennials**

*Sun becomes sugar,*
*Root becomes stem,*
*Light becomes energy;*
*Who told them?*

Me, I can't even sleep right. Natural things don't come to me.
I don't breathe right. I can't sing; my sister, a voice teacher, says it's because
of the way I breathe.
A woman who the paper said had taught more than 10,000 people to swim at the Jewish Community Center couldn't teach me. She said it was because I don't breathe right.

Every blade and vein, every bug and bee knows what they're here for.
And for that they have my great admiration.
The worm sliding silently through its clod, safe in its shiny slime,
showing off its perfect, pink segments, is filled with business and purpose, thank you,
no hurry, nothing to see here, doing it all for God.
Disassembling stuff. Making hard stuff crumbly and useful.

> *Bud becomes bloom,*
> *Seed becomes shoot;*
> *Energy extends the root.*

I get up at daylight to answer my garden's call, grab a trowel and yank weeds.
On the back porch, the spider's filaments stretch 'til they reach just the right place,
and then stick,
while I myself spin and ricochet, unknowing when to stop
or where I'm supposed to be going.
And now the raindrops, starting as ice, cheerfully fall, changing into their wet destiny.
I'm sure each one is shouting, "Whee!"
Everybody gets it but me.

At the roses, I rise,
press my aching back, and wonder.
The leaf and the lawn of it—
the moth and the fly—
everyone knows what they're doing, but I—

I, the gardener—just muck around in the dirt and rocks,
worms and slugs,
mud and bugs.

My grampa came here in steerage from Lithuania, a Jew despised.
But over the crown of Liberty, he said, the sun's setting rays beamed on his
    boat.
Then his own son rose, a success, and now I, that son's daughter,
have earned the mantle of the family disappointment.
I kind of went through college, didn't quite know why; never had that
    "dream"
the graduation speakers tell you to follow. I liked writing, but
certainly didn't "dream" of it; might have tried teaching, but couldn't stand
    the word,
"pedagogy." It didn't rhyme with anything, it had no sense of humor,
and the course descriptions all sounded so … pedagogical.
Not to mention that there wasn't anything
I knew enough about to teach.
When these leaves turn red, I'll be 70,
and I still haven't declared my major.

When I go, shred and compost me; not to fester, but to feed. To be of use. Not
    to rot
in a box in a concrete vault, but to do my sweet decay, and in doing so, finally
    to join
the dance, properly and in my place, right where I belong.
Plant me among the native American perennials; it'll be my way of thanking
    grampa
for his long, hard trip.
Lay me near the alley where crabgrass, plantain and spurge break the
bluestone walks and every unkempt curb sprouts wild mustard, Queen
Anne's lace, and chicory – the yellow, white and blue banners of my beloved
    summers.
Dig me into the tough, plain stuff, the ones with the awful names: pigweed,
stinkweed, milkweed, poke. Let them have the last laugh at God's old joke.

They'll be back in the spring, knowing why.
And maybe—who knows?—so will I.

**Late-Winter Cryptography**

Mark the white lines in bark when snow is upon it.
Unseen 'til now, they disappear again as thick
ghost-globs drop to the root-rich ground. Be quick,
or you'll miss this evanescent sonnet.

Green-gowned boughs hold cotton-puff trays:
"Look at me!" the cedars say, and leave us branching for words.
(They don't just pose, as in rainy green days
when they ached, yet carried nothing but birds.)

Blue shadows mirroring the sky in hollowed banks
where shovel-scoops are dug, hug heart,
brain, and eye alike, joining what's apart.
Listen, for they all proffer thanks.

A red ash berry doffs its jaunty cloud-cap;
each peach bud makes a brittle little clap.
Crystal crunch of ice-veneer shatters on your wrap;
silver sleeves on frosty twigs glitter, drip, and snap.

Scan the silent stanzas for still sacred signs
in a code that summer's soldiers cannot crack.
In the grip of this encryption, for the wise they leave a tip:
Hearken to the white around the black.

**Forward March**

Daffodils are waving; spring's contract has been signed.
A crocus calls out, giggling, to others of its kind
as cheerful blooms in triumph above the earth erupt;
scents of purple heaven among new leaves are cupped.

And yet this March is maddening. We shrivel in surprise,
startled by the bluster as bitter winds arise.
A warning: Warmer weather can pivot like a mood.
Tomorrow's grim is looming; the forecast force is lewd.

Now go, retrieve the salt from off the basement mound!
Shovels must be readied; scarves again be found,
and booted as before, we'll lift our wipers high—
a salute to Sergeant Winter from our own Private July.

**Relief**

Robins spring across the bluff;
the woodchucks waddle after.
Now is the laughter-time, when stuff
from cottonwoods, all closed and tough,
bursts into white confetti-fluff.

The weather, done rehearsing, sings
a softer, saner tune.
Soon comes the June of joy, that flings
our cares like heavy coats and things,
and frees our bright imaginings.

The wind surrenders and retreats;
fists and hearts unwind.
And now the mind, as well, defeats
every dreary thought it meets.
The world continues and completes.

**None of Us in Nineveh**

None of us in Nineveh could fathom what he meant.
Neither sage nor wit, he came to our great city
from some puny Podunk—sent, he said, by God.
And still, he stank of rotting fish
and brought a loony tale that he'd been swallowed.

No one followed his mad rambling. Most of us
were gambling his brains had broiled in sand and sun
and never would recover. It's happened to others.
We made circles with a finger by our ears,
and rolled our eyes. Here are the whys:
Jonah said that God would bring us down—
Capital of Assyria, mind you, and here this clown
swore God would overthrow us. (Many mighty armies tried,
and ended fried on spits). Still, something in his manic message,
half-drowned inside us, was gnawing at our wits:
Maybe we'd all gone overboard with the cruelty and violence. So we fasted,
not to see how long we lasted, but for real. Now, here's the deal:
Forty days came and went, and this God of Jonah's
must have liked our grand repent,
for nothing happened. Yet Jonah, spent, seemed sad,
instead of being glad for us. He cried
and said when God forgave us, he wished that he had died.

He was only angry his prediction turned out wrong
(and it's true that with hilarity he'll be remembered long).
A squash grew up above him, on the hill, giving shade,
and he briefly stopped his bawling,
but then it withered really quick and started falling,
and we heard him wail once more as he sat there like a fool—
but we Ninevites, for God's sake, find forgiveness really cool.

**Against Roses**

The ruby red of the red, red rose
bores me, with its trite perfume
so redolent of musty prose
that long ago has lost its bloom.
Its prickles, in a sharp surprise,
perform a bloody exercise.

How tiresome to adopt the guise
of praising gardens' garnet queen
while from the curb, the chicories rise,
their brilliant rays so clearly seen,
and in the ditch, that batch of blues
and sturdy stems with summer fuse.

To some a weed more than a muse
(and spurned among the spotted spurges),
the dandelion shouts, "Refuse
to do what cold convention urges!
Put down your pampered, pretty gift,
and to the tough all praises lift."

**Summer Run**

August road, newly paved.
Its clean, pure black calls you: Run.

White daisies with yellow yolks nod while
tiny bluets peek from prickly leaves of dock.
The shoulder's flat and sandy—level, almost, with the road.
Black and yellow butterflies float alongside, crazy
as dry leaves in wind. And yet they keep up.
Perhaps they like the sounds of water in the plastic bottle sloshing
and feet drumming asphalt in this hypnotic slap-slap-slap.
The whole world is humming—wires above, cicadas below.
Crunchy insects and dried-out worms punctuate the path;
my own hot sweat-drops resolve into runnels around them.

Rubber soles fusing with hot tar
and creosote seeping from phone-poles: the scents of summer.
Squiggles of heat shimmer over the road.
Stone pillars, top of hill: Goal!

Coming back, trees crowd the slanted road-edge
and fern-feathers shade the mud. But even the mud is hot.
Peer into puddles for tadpoles and toads: not today.
Chipmunks on the rocks mimic bird-chirps ten yards deep
in the dark-green woods. So inviting, but: Don't stop.
Lower your head and push.
Laurel blossoms cup for moisture, receiving none.
A sudden caterpillar dangles by its invisible thread, face-level: Spit him out!
And keep going. Broken, brown beer bottle: Lengthen your stride to miss it.
Uphill again, and breath comes harder. Try to reach that fallen branch
without stopping. Come on: You can do it. Do it. Do it.

Done! Skid down the short, pebbly bank and span the ditch, heading for
    shade.
Hands on knees, wincing and panting under the trees, look up and
squeeze water into your mouth, over your neck and down the front of your
    shirt.
And smile: Soon enough you'll be old, and winter will be here,
and you won't even remember this branch,
these birds, that ditch, those bugs,
this summer run.

## Silly Sonnet

The sonnet doesn't lend itself to mirth;
its topics are ennobling and profound.
It's love and youth, redemption and rebirth
that Shakespeare built his honored verse around.
So train your mind to contemplate pure beauty
or truth for inspiration. Since it seems
that gaining wisdom is one's highest duty,
reject the low for any sonnet's themes.
No flatulence must ruin their aroma;
no boogers green upon their words must stick;
no knock-knock jokes to put us in a coma,
no puerile puns; no adolescent shtick.
Will Shakespeare set the bar, so follow Willy,
and never write a sonnet that is silly.

**Doing the Dishes with my Father**

I'm standing in front of the sink holding a dishrag under a
slow trickle of hot water, the drops as evenly spaced as paratroopers
leaping from a helicopter. And now I'm swirling the rag
around the inside of the pasta pot like a scout swinging
binoculars in an arc across a dense, booby-trapped forest,
and all the while, I'm singing with my father, the way he used to sing
his Army songs to us, when we were all very little, not long after the war.

He never made it overseas; he remained at Fort Dix writing stories for
Stars and Stripes. Back home, he had three kids pretty quick, and taught us
his songs. He sang them while driving, cooking, playing with us
in the yard and always, while doing the dishes. I washed; he wiped.
He edited his songs on the fly, dropping dirty words like Nazis in an M1 scope
and substituting good, clean, American words.
"Mademoiselle from Armentiers, she hasn't been loved in a hundred years," he'd sing,
and we'd join in on the "Inky-dinky parlez-vous." Or he'd sing: "You're in the Army now;
you're not behind the plow. / You son of a gun, you'll never get rich; / You're in the Army now."
He belted out those songs with such gusto, sometimes doing a little soft-shoe at the same time,
you'd think he'd been a general, instead of the oldest buck private in New Jersey.
He died thirty years ago last fall; that's a long time to be AWOL.

But now my husband comes up behind me to give me a hug over the dishpan,
and to ask what the heck I was singing. Waving the soapy flag of our battalion,
I about-face and reply in the key of C:
"This is the Army, Mister Jones; / no private rooms or telephones ..."
All kindness, he let me cry against his chest;
I just wish people wouldn't bother me when I'm doing the dishes with my father.

**But the Trees**

We all go the same way in the heat of the day—
in the wilt, the scorch, the fry.
Everyone crosses the street for shade—
the heroes, the homeless and I.
    **But the trees:**
The trees at the curb will never disturb
us; instead, they stolidly stand
with leaves and roots that clean and cool
our water, air and land.
We're making our nation a dry desperation
of dust, drought and fire.
Rain on the walk now turns to steam
as the temperature climbs higher.
    **But the trees:**
Their gracious green shelter combats the swelter—
quells carbon, wind and storms,
bestowing us beauty as well as relief
as the place that we love ever warms.
Oh, it comes at a cost, the smog and exhaust—
we cough and choke and wheeze,
but trees keep us alive, so if we survive,
we'll have none else to thank but the trees.

**Come Sit on the Porch**

Come sit on the porch with me, my love,
while the world falls apart.
A tumorous cloud at the river rises rapid,
like milk boiling over a too-small pan.
It emerges enorming, forming a storm
as unique steam startles and enrages it.

And now look: The whole sky is a color I've never seen.
It begins to go a blackish green.
While the wind whips the brackish waves, sailors scatter
and fishers flee for the nearest dock.
Why feign shock? This is what we have made for ourselves.
The world has turned on us, as we have turned on the world.

Rain is pelting the melting streets (not cooling—just angry).
Outside, the sun fried us all morning; now a torrent keens
and screams. There seems no air.
We are poaching; we are boiling.
Shall we suffocate, or drown?
Shall we suffocate, or drown? Come sit down
and drink, my love, a toast
to the end of the world.

**The Rights of Nature**

They're starting to talk of the Rights of Nature. They're starting to sue.
They're saying that trees—trees! And animals of all kinds,
even the kinds we don't like, the beetles, the ants, the rats, all of them—
and then the seasons, the seas, the weathers, the lakes, the rivers and oceans—
all of Nature, they're saying,
has Rights. We used to think only people did. We're certainly proud of ours:
We write poems, anthems, briefs and more about our Rights.
We fight and die for them. We get choked up about them.
All humans, born and unborn, we declare, have Rights, no matter how or when those humans got
or ever will get created, intentionally or unintentionally—no matter what their happiness
or misery is likely to be—no matter what their mothers bore or can bear.
Meanwhile, the Mother of us all, Nature—which all of life is and depends on,
exists, we say, for us to plunder, so we can make more plastic, more
weapons, more stuff, more money. Those of us drained of our melanin
for G-d only knows what ancient crimes have always claimed parts of the
planet as "ours," and once our flag is planted somewhere, we claim we can
destroy that part as we wish. We chop down her trees, drill her, extract
her insides and bury plastic in her, uncaring that the birds we love and the
plants we need, all fed and pollinated
by those creepy, itchy insects, are leaving us—
leaving us with no clean air, no clean water; no water at all.

"All yours," they're saying. "Goodbye. Enjoy the heat."
The First Peoples tried to tell us that the earth isn't ours.
They were uncomprehending when we People of Pallor came and declared
that we "owned" the dirt, the forests, the hunting grounds and the good
planting places. But we cheated and poisoned the First Peoples, and now it
seems it may be too late to listen to them.
Our children, depressed or horrified, are asking us, "What have you done?"
But now some of them, few but a mighty few, are claiming
that they are silent Nature's spokespeople and trustees. Trustees! Legally responsible
for the health and welfare of trees! Of dirt! Of water and air!
They're starting to talk about the Rights of Nature.
And they're starting to sue.

**Genie Abrams**, author of the novels *Louey Levy's Greatest Catch*, *Louey Levy's Perfect Pitch*, and *Louey Levy's Heading Home*, is a former journalist and public-relations director for a variety of local, statewide and national nonprofits. She served a term on Newburgh's City Council but is out on parole. For fun, she gardens and picks up trash in the 'hood. She was the Poet Laureate of Newburgh from 2022-2024. Her favorite poets are A.E. Stallings and Billy Collins. Reach her at genieabrams@gmail.com.